Nightwritten

Peetha van der Veen

BookLeaf
Publishing

India | USA | UK

Presentation by *BookLeaf Publishing*

Web: www.bookleafpub.com

E-mail: info@bookleafpub.com

ISBN: 978-93-5744-462-0

First edition 2022

DEDICATION

For those that helped me see the stars in a blank night sky.

Dreaming of Stars

We used to watch the stars together
Dreaming of bigger things
In our minds we'd explore the skies
On imaginary wings
We'd see the cheering audience
And stand on an invisible stage
I thought this friendship would last forever
But we grew apart with age
I lost you then, I watched you go
As from this magic you were torn away
I was happy in this fantasy
And when you left I could only stay
See once upon a time you were a dreamer
Living in this beautiful world inside your head
Now you're faking smiles and working all day
Your only refuge these sleepless nights in bed
Your world could have been a mirror of mine
Magical, bright and full of life
But you let go; you forgot
And now you're walking on the edge of a knife
But know that there is light at the end of the
tunnel
That you can't see the rainbow without the rain
Know that while you may feel trapped in a
world of grays

Hope is not lost; and this color you can regain
So when you wake from your nightmare reality
Join me in the dream world of mine
And once you recall what it's like to wonder
Keep that memory close and you'll be just fine
When you reminisce on our younger days
And look up at the night sky
When again you wish upon that shooting star
Remember us and wave me goodbye

darkness/shadows

Do you see how when you run
From the shadows in your head
The darkness is all that can hide you?
But it is only shadows spread

Sacrifice? Enemy?

You could see it in their eyes:
With your downfall they would rise

chaos

5

You walk with chaos all around
Where you go this world bleeds

But who knows? Maybe
It's just chaos that this world needs

Lost and Found

You might think you'll never come back
That you've strayed too far from the trail
You might feel too far away
Like an old love letter lost in the mail
You might feel forgotten in the forest
Hidden in the trees
But before you can walk home
You have to get up off your knees
You may seem to be unreachable
Or simply gone too long
But sometimes you have to be weak
Before you can be strong
It's like that saying we've all heard of
That quote that we all know
It tells us what would happen should we
In a certain direction go
Because what goes up
Must come down
And what is lost
Can only be found

And Then

And then the light drained from your eyes
Like softened, silenced battlecries

not

As crimson drips down to the floor
A mind and body long at war
You hear a whispered voice so frail
Then drops of blood turn to a trail

Her Goodbye

When this feeling around us dies
And the starlight reflects in her eyes
There is nothing I can do but
Watch as silently she cries

When fire within her no longer rages
As it has throughout the ages
I feel that I am then surrounded;
Trapped as if by a thousand cages

When all her colors turn to shades
Of gray; like long-forgotten blades
The sight tears me to pieces
When from her eyes that bright spark fades

When she departs from this world of waking
I learn what it's like to feel yourself breaking
I feel myself shatter and a piece
With her, to darkness, she is taking

One Day

One day there'll be no words left in
The dictionary to describe
The way you feel about someone
The way you feel inside

Dreamers

Why should I give up this world
I see inside my head?
What reason do I have
To get up and out of bed?
Why would you force me back to reality
Where I have no lucky charm?
What right do you have to wake me
When in my dreams I am calm?
Why do you tear me away
From this gentle paradise?
A heaven only I know
That you dare to compromise.
I should have known you'd never stop
And let me rest alone,
Yet rousing me is a crime
For which you should atone.
Why can you never leave me
To be myself as I wish?
Why do you take it upon yourself
To keep me from the place I relish?
Why should I follow you into the waking world
When all I want from it is distance?
For the only thing that can kill a dreamer
Is the reminder of their own existence

One Storm

This storm that raged above us all
Left even giants feeling small
It brought down all of humankind
This storm that waged inside your mind

Re-

Even when from this world we're torn
I'll never not find you
Because of the same star we're born
And born we'll be anew

A Language Lost

The trees they whisper to me
In a language lost to most
They speak to me in words you'll never know
For you've forgotten these ancient tongues

These streams sing ballads of long ago
Tales in foreign words
They mourn the lost and praise the heroes
But you'll never understand

This land chants a constant poem
But it doesn't take a dreamer to know
The hum of the earth without a reply
Is only background noise

The tides harmonize
But the melodies are twisted
And the sounds are strange in your mind like
Snow in a raging fire

The wind warns of soon misfortunes
And guides you with an ancestor's grave
Yet you won't feel the danger near
With your senses so long dulled

This heartbeat echoes voices of the past
But the words reach deafened ears
For only those that listen can
Translate a language lost

'gone'

Like some kind of tragic song
You're worn this mask for far too long
Your true face no one would recognise
You've disappeared from the world's eyes

Walls of Glass

You broke down all the walls
She'd built as a protective cage
You tore down her guard, and with it, her spirit
Letting her believe a lie
You watch calmly as her tears flowed
In shimmering streams down her face
You laughed as her heart crumbled to pieces
And left her there alone
You ignored her cries and calls for help
And simply walked away
You built her up
Just to break her down
You stole her freedom
And made her fight
You destroyed her
To make her stronger
You shattered her walls of glass
And taught her to build them of stone

[Contradiction]

Sometimes I lie awake at night
Because sleep is tiring
Sometimes I wish the dark would come
But instead lay there crying
Sometimes I want the day to end
So I may see the stars
Sometimes I wish for nothing more
Than a pink-orange sunrise

Tear; Stream; Flood

Like raindrops from the sky I fall
Looking for a place to land
I want only to hear the call
That tells me where you stand

Creature

It's gold as light through forest leaves
And cold as wind through mountains weaves
It holds a power over you
Its strength and strike are always true
You cannot tell if it is light
Or a darkness made of spite
Sometimes you wish to see its face
Although the thought makes your heart race
You know that it cannot be beat
This thing you only wish to meet
You know that it cannot be good
Shrouded in shadows like a hood
Yet you can't seem to walk away
Its mystery makes your heart sway
It's far too big yet feels so small
It is nothing; it is all

'Sorry?'

You could apologize
In a thousand languages
And still I doubt I could forgive you

Starnights

Sometimes we need the night to see
How bright the stars can truly be

You; Stars

I said once that stars are beautiful
But I wouldn't watch them without you
Because like a world without you in it
Stars can be lonely, too